"The Power of Voice: Lawyer in a Black Coat,"

Swatantra Bahadur

Published by Swatantra Bahadur, 2023.

While every precaution has been taken in the preparation of this book, the publisher assumes no responsibility for errors or omissions, or for damages resulting from the use of the information contained herein.

"THE POWER OF VOICE: LAWYER IN A BLACK COAT,"

First edition. October 8, 2023.

Copyright © 2023 Swatantra Bahadur.

ISBN: 979-8223916987

Written by Swatantra Bahadur.

Disclaimer

THE INFORMATION PRESENTED in this book is intended for general informational purposes only and should not be relied upon as a substitute for professional advice or judgment. The author and publisher are not responsible for any action taken by readers based on the information provided in this book. Readers should seek appropriate professional advice or conduct their own research before making decisions related to the topics discussed in this book. The views expressed in this book are those of the author and do not necessarily reflect the views of the publisher.

Contents

Introduction

In the hallowed halls of the legal world, where justice is meted out, and the balance of society is preserved, there exists an enigmatic figure: the lawyer in a black coat. While this emblematic attire may seem like a mere sartorial choice, it conceals within its folds a formidable source of power—the power of voice. This book, "The Power of Voice: Lawyer in a Black Coat," ventures into the heart of this legal mystique, unearthing the profound influence that a lawyer's voice wields in the corridors of justice, in the realm of negotiation, and in the wider landscape of public discourse.

Imagine a courtroom where the verdict hangs in the balance, where truth teeters on the precipice, and where the scales of justice sway with each carefully chosen word. In this crucible of law, a lawyer's voice is not just a conduit for argument; it is a formidable tool capable of reshaping destinies, of tipping the scales one way or the other, and of swaying the minds of judges and juries. Whether it's the rhythmic cadence of a closing statement, the unwavering tone of cross-examination, or the eloquent appeal to a jury's conscience, the voice of a lawyer has the power to persuade, to inspire, and to change lives.

"The Power of Voice: Lawyer in a Black Coat" embarks on a journey through the multifaceted world of legal advocacy, from the classical art of oratory that has shaped legal history to the cutting-edge techniques used in modern courtrooms. It delves into the psychology of persuasion, revealing the subtle techniques that lawyers employ to win cases, and explores the ethical boundaries that govern the use of persuasive speech in the pursuit of justice.

But the lawyer's voice transcends the courtroom. It echoes through the chambers of negotiation, where settlements are brokered and disputes resolved. It resonates in the public eye, as lawyers engage in public speaking engagements, media appearances, and the creation of personal brands. This book examines how a lawyer's voice extends beyond the confines of litigation and how it can be harnessed to create lasting impact and influence.

Yet, the journey to becoming a master of voice in the legal profession is not without its challenges. Lawyers must navigate the delicate balance between assertiveness and professionalism, while also overcoming common hurdles in vocal confidence and clarity. This book provides practical guidance and exercises to help lawyers refine their voices and amplify their persuasive abilities.

In an era of rapid technological change and evolving communication platforms, the legal profession is not immune to transformation. "The Power of Voice" contemplates the future of legal advocacy, considering the role of artificial intelligence, the impact of diversity and inclusion, and the need for adaptation in a shifting landscape.

As we embark on this exploration of the lawyer's voice, we invite you to uncover the secrets, strategies, and stories that have shaped legal advocacy throughout history. Whether you are a practicing lawyer seeking to enhance your skills or a curious observer intrigued by the power of voice, this book offers insights, inspiration, and a deeper understanding of the indomitable force concealed within the black coat.

A. HOOK - ANECDOTE or statistic about the impact of a lawyer's voice in the courtroom

A courtroom, the epitome of solemnity and high-stakes drama, often witnesses the transformative power of a lawyer's voice. Consider the case of Emily Patterson, a young attorney defending a wrongfully accused defendant in a murder trial. The odds were stacked against her client, the evidence seemingly insurmountable. But as Emily stood before the jury, her voice, measured and unwavering, began to weave a narrative that would alter the course of justice.

In the final moments of her closing argument, Emily's voice, filled with conviction, delivered a single sentence that hung in the air like an irrefutable truth: "Ladies and gentlemen of the jury, you hold not only the life of my client in your hands, but the very essence of justice itself." The hushed courtroom, once a cauldron of doubt, was now gripped by her words. The jury, transfixed by the power of her voice, would later return with a verdict of "not guilty."

This anecdote illustrates just one of countless instances where a lawyer's voice has turned the tide of justice, where words spoken with precision and passion became the difference between imprisonment and freedom. The power of a lawyer's voice is more than mere eloquence; it is the catalyst for profound change in the lives of individuals and the very fabric of society itself.

B. PURPOSE OF THE BOOK - To explore the profound influence of a lawyer's voice in the legal profession.

The purpose of this book, "The Power of Voice: Lawyer in a Black Coat," is to embark on a comprehensive exploration of the profound and often underestimated influence of a lawyer's voice in the legal profession. In the corridors of justice, the power of voice is not a mere tool; it is the linchpin that can sway verdicts, forge settlements, and shape the course of legal proceedings. This book seeks to delve deeply into this phenomenon, unraveling the layers of significance that a lawyer's voice carries, and shedding light on the nuanced ways in which it impacts the legal world. Through in-depth analysis, case studies, and expert insights, this book aims to achieve the following objectives:

Uncover the Art of Oratory: Delve into the history and evolution of oratory as a foundational skill in the legal profession. Explore how great legal orators of the past have influenced the course of justice and how these skills continue to be relevant in contemporary legal practice.

Reveal the Psychology of Persuasion: Examine the psychology behind persuasive communication and its profound relevance in the legal context. Investigate the strategies and techniques lawyers employ to persuade judges, juries, clients, and opponents.

Ethical Considerations: Discuss the ethical boundaries of persuasive speech in law, addressing questions of fairness, honesty, and the responsibility of lawyers to uphold the principles of justice while using their voices to advocate for their clients.

Extend Beyond the Courtroom: Explore how a lawyer's voice extends its influence to negotiation, mediation, public speaking engagements, and media appearances. Investigate how effective communication can be a critical factor in achieving favorable outcomes in legal matters.

Address Challenges and Enhance Skills: Provide practical guidance and exercises for lawyers to improve their vocal confidence, clarity, and persuasiveness. Address common challenges lawyers face in honing their communication skills.

Anticipate the Future: Contemplate the evolving landscape of legal advocacy in an era of technological advancements and changing communication platforms. Consider the role of artificial intelligence, diversity and inclusion, and the need for adaptation in the legal profession.

Inspire and Educate: Ultimately, this book aims to inspire legal professionals to harness the full potential of their voices and educate both lawyers and the broader public about the pivotal role of voice in the pursuit of justice.

By delving into these facets of a lawyer's voice, this book seeks to offer valuable insights, practical advice, and a deeper understanding of the enduring power that lies within the black coat and the voices that emanate from it. Through these explorations, it is our hope that readers will gain a newfound appreciation for the art of advocacy and the transformative influence of a lawyer's voice in the legal profession and society at large.

II. The Legal World Unveiled

In the opening chapter of "The Power of Voice: Lawyer in a Black Coat," titled "The Legal World Unveiled," we embark on a journey to demystify the intricate and often enigmatic realm of the legal profession. This chapter serves as a foundational introduction to the overarching theme of the book: the profound influence of a lawyer's voice in the legal arena.

I. Introduction to the Legal Realm

This section establishes the context by defining the essential role of lawyers in society. It paints a vivid picture of lawyers as multifaceted professionals who not only advocate for their clients but also serve as counselors and interpreters of the law. The chapter highlights how lawyers are integral to upholding justice and maintaining the rule of law, making decisions with far-reaching implications for individuals and society as a whole.

II. The Power of Attire: The Black Coat and Beyond

Here, the chapter delves into the symbolic and historical significance of the black coat, which is a hallmark of lawyers' attire. It explores how attire serves as a non-verbal form of communication and influences perceptions of authority, trustworthiness, and professionalism within the legal field. By discussing the choice of attire, the section underscores the gravity and solemnity of legal proceedings.

III. Effective Communication in the Legal Profession

This section emphasizes the paramount importance of effective communication skills in the legal profession. It elucidates that lawyers often deal with complex legal concepts that need to be conveyed in a comprehensible manner to various stakeholders, including clients, judges, and juries. The consequences of poor communication within legal practice, such as misinterpretation and a loss of trust, are also highlighted.

IV. The Power of Voice as a Tool of Influence

The chapter then transitions into its central theme—the influence of a lawyer's voice. It explains how a lawyer's voice serves as their primary instrument for conveying arguments, building credibility, and persuading others in the legal world. It introduces anecdotes and statistics to underscore the impact of a persuasive voice in legal settings, setting the stage for a deeper exploration of this theme in the subsequent chapters.

V. The Promise of the Black Coat: A Preview of What's to Come

In the final section of the chapter, readers are given a glimpse of the journey ahead. It previews the subsequent chapters, indicating that the book will delve into the art of oratory, the psychology of persuasion, ethical considerations within the legal profession, and more. It encourages readers to embark on this exploration, promising a deeper understanding of the multifaceted role of a lawyer's voice in the pursuit of justice.

Overall, "The Legal World Unveiled" sets the stage for the reader by providing a solid foundation in understanding the significance of lawyers and their communication skills in the legal profession. It lays the groundwork for the in-depth exploration of the power of a lawyer's voice in the chapters that follow, inviting readers to uncover the hidden intricacies of the legal world.

A. DEFINITION OF A Lawyer's Role in Society

A lawyer, often referred to as an attorney, plays a multifaceted and essential role in society as a legal professional entrusted with upholding the principles of justice, safeguarding the rule of law, and advocating for the rights and interests of individuals and entities. Their role encompasses various key responsibilities and functions:

1. Advocate for Clients:

Lawyers serve as advocates for their clients, whether they are individuals, businesses, or organizations. They provide legal representation by presenting their clients' interests, arguments, and legal positions in a court of law or other legal settings. This advocacy includes conducting legal research, preparing legal documents, and arguing cases on behalf of their clients.

2. Counsel and Adviser:

Lawyers offer legal advice and counsel to their clients. They interpret complex legal statutes, regulations, and precedents to help clients understand their rights and responsibilities. Attorneys provide guidance on potential legal issues, strategies for addressing them, and the implications of various legal courses of action.

3. Interpreters of the Law:

Lawyers are responsible for interpreting and applying the law. They ensure that their clients' actions comply with applicable laws and regulations and provide insights into how the law affects specific situations. Lawyers help bridge the gap between legal complexities and their practical implications.

4. Guardians of Due Process:

Lawyers play a vital role in safeguarding due process and ensuring that legal proceedings are fair and just. They uphold the principles of equity and impartiality by advocating for the rights of their clients and ensuring that legal proceedings adhere to established legal norms and procedures.

5. Mediators and Negotiators:

Lawyers often serve as mediators and negotiators, working to resolve disputes through alternative methods such as negotiation, mediation, or arbitration. They aim to find mutually acceptable solutions for their clients without resorting to lengthy and costly court battles.

6. Public Advocates:

Some lawyers engage in public interest work, advocating for broader societal issues, civil rights, or the welfare of marginalized communities. They may work for non-profit organizations, governmental agencies, or engage in pro bono legal work to promote justice and the common good.

7. Officers of the Court:

Lawyers are considered officers of the court and are expected to uphold ethical standards and professional conduct. They have a responsibility to ensure that justice is served and that the legal system functions efficiently and fairly.

8. Legal Educators and Scholars:

Many lawyers become legal educators, teaching aspiring lawyers about the law, ethics, and legal practice. Some lawyers also engage in legal scholarship, conducting research and contributing to the development of legal theory and jurisprudence.

In summary, a lawyer's role in society is multifaceted and crucial. They serve as advocates, counselors, interpreters of the law, and guardians of due process, working to ensure that justice is served, rights are protected, and the rule of law is upheld. Whether representing individual clients, corporations, or public interests, lawyers are instrumental in maintaining the fabric of a just and orderly society.

B. THE IMPORTANCE OF Effective Communication Skills in the Legal Profession

Effective communication skills are the lifeblood of the legal profession, serving as the cornerstone of a lawyer's ability to succeed in their role. Here are some key reasons why these skills are of paramount importance:

Advocacy in Court: Lawyers must present compelling arguments and advocate persuasively in court. This involves not only knowing the law but also effectively communicating it to judges and juries. The ability to articulate complex legal concepts clearly and convincingly can make the difference between winning and losing a case.

Client Relationships: Lawyers need to build strong relationships with their clients, gaining their trust and confidence. Effective communication is essential for understanding clients' needs, explaining legal options, and managing expectations. Clients rely on lawyers to translate legal jargon into understandable terms.

Negotiation and Mediation: Many legal matters are resolved through negotiation or mediation rather than litigation. Lawyers must communicate effectively with opposing counsel and other parties to reach mutually beneficial agreements. Effective negotiation skills can lead to favorable settlements and avoid protracted legal battles.

Legal Writing: Legal documents, such as contracts, briefs, and motions, require precise and clear writing. Effective legal writing is crucial for drafting agreements, making legal arguments, and conveying complex legal issues to judges and other parties.

Persuasion and Argumentation: Lawyers often need to persuade judges, juries, or opposing parties of the validity of their positions. Persuasive communication involves not only the content of arguments but also the tone, delivery, and presentation. A well-delivered argument can sway opinions and influence outcomes.

Conflict Resolution: Lawyers frequently deal with conflicts, whether in litigation, family law, or business disputes. Effective communication is vital for de-escalating conflicts, resolving differences, and finding common ground among parties with competing interests.

Ethical Considerations: Lawyers have ethical responsibilities to communicate honestly and transparently with clients, opposing parties, and the court. Violations of ethical standards related to communication can lead to professional misconduct and legal consequences.

Public Speaking and Presentations: Lawyers often engage in public speaking, whether in courtrooms, boardrooms, or public forums. Effective oral communication skills are necessary for presenting cases, delivering speeches, and representing clients in various settings.

Credibility and Trust: Lawyers must establish credibility and trust with judges, clients, and colleagues. Effective communication fosters confidence in the lawyer's abilities and professionalism, which is essential for a successful legal career.

Conflict of Interest Avoidance: Lawyers must communicate potential conflicts of interest to clients and other parties transparently. Failure to do so can lead to legal malpractice claims and damage to professional reputation.

In essence, the legal profession relies heavily on effective communication skills to navigate a complex web of legal matters, build relationships, resolve disputes, and ensure that justice is served. Lawyers who excel in communication not only enhance their own success but also contribute to the fair and efficient functioning of the legal system.

C. THE SYMBOLISM OF the Black Coat and Its Historical Significance

The black coat, often donned by lawyers, is a symbol with deep historical and cultural significance in the legal profession. Its symbolism extends beyond mere fashion, and it carries a weight of tradition and professionalism. Here's an exploration of the historical significance and symbolism associated with the black coat worn by lawyers:

1. Tradition and Formality:

Historically, lawyers have worn black coats to signify their commitment to tradition, formality, and seriousness in the practice of law. Black has long been associated with dignity and solemnity, traits expected of legal professionals in their roles as officers of the court.

2. Historical Roots:

The tradition of wearing black attire can be traced back to the 17th century in England. Lawyers in the United Kingdom began wearing black robes as a way to mourn the death of Queen Mary II. This tradition later evolved to become a symbol of professionalism and respect for the legal process.

3. Impartiality and Neutrality:

The black coat signifies the lawyer's commitment to impartiality and neutrality. It represents the idea that lawyers are advocates for their clients but are also bound by ethical and professional duties to uphold the principles of justice and fairness.

4. Role in Courtroom Dramatics:

In the courtroom, the black coat serves as a visual symbol of authority and expertise. When lawyers stand before judges, juries, and clients, their attire underscores the seriousness of legal proceedings and the weight of the decisions being made.

5. Uniformity and Equality:

Wearing black coats in court helps create a sense of uniformity among legal professionals. Regardless of their background or personal style, lawyers present a unified front when advocating for their clients. This sense of equality under the law is reinforced by the consistent attire.

6. Legal Education:

In many legal education institutions, law students are introduced to the tradition of wearing black coats early in their training. This serves as a rite of passage, signifying their entry into the legal profession and the responsibilities that come with it.

7. Global Recognition:

The tradition of wearing black attire has transcended national borders and is recognized worldwide as a symbol of the legal profession. It is a visual cue that instantly identifies an individual as a lawyer, regardless of language or cultural differences.

8. Connection to Legal History:

The black coat is a link to the rich history of the legal profession. Lawyers today continue to honor and uphold the traditions established by their predecessors, fostering a sense of continuity and respect for the rule of law.

In summary, the black coat worn by lawyers holds profound historical and symbolic significance. It represents a commitment to tradition, formality, impartiality, and the solemnity of the legal profession. It is a visual reminder of the lawyer's role as an advocate for justice and a guardian of the legal system's integrity. The black coat serves as a unifying symbol that transcends borders and languages, connecting lawyers to their legal heritage and their shared responsibility to uphold the principles of law and justice.

III. The Art of Oratory

The art of oratory is a skillful and persuasive form of public speaking characterized by the ability to engage, captivate, and influence an audience through the effective use of spoken language and rhetorical techniques. Oratory is not merely about conveying information; it is about crafting and delivering speeches in a compelling and impactful manner that leaves a lasting impression on listeners. The art of oratory encompasses several key elements:

Rhetorical Techniques: Oratory involves the skillful use of rhetorical devices such as metaphors, similes, analogies, and alliteration to enhance the beauty and power of speech. Rhetorical techniques are employed strategically to make arguments more persuasive and memorable.

Emotional Appeal: Effective oratory taps into the emotions of the audience, evoking empathy, sympathy, or passion. It aims to connect with listeners on an emotional level, making them more receptive to the speaker's message.

Clarity and Conciseness: Oratory emphasizes clear and concise communication. Complex ideas are presented in a straightforward manner, ensuring that the audience can easily grasp and follow the speaker's arguments.

Voice and Delivery: The delivery of an orator is a crucial aspect. This includes aspects such as tone, pace, volume, and intonation. A skilled orator modulates their voice to match the content and context of their speech, enhancing its impact.

Body Language and Gestures: Oratory is not limited to spoken words alone; it also encompasses non-verbal communication. Effective orators use gestures, facial expressions, and body language to complement and reinforce their spoken message.

Organization and Structure: Oratory requires careful structuring of content. Speeches typically follow a clear organizational pattern, which may include an introduction, body, and conclusion. Each section serves a specific purpose in advancing the speaker's argument.

Audience Awareness: A successful orator tailors their speech to the needs and expectations of their audience. They consider the audience's knowledge, beliefs, and values, adjusting their message accordingly to maximize its impact.

Historical Significance: Throughout history, oratory has played a pivotal role in shaping public opinion, inciting change, and inspiring movements. Famous orators like Martin Luther King Jr., Winston Churchill, and Cicero are celebrated for their ability to use the art of oratory to effect change and leave a lasting legacy.

The art of oratory is not limited to public speaking on grand stages but is also relevant in various contexts, including legal arguments, political discourse, business presentations, and motivational speeches. Skilled orators have the power to sway opinions, mobilize support, and convey complex ideas with clarity and persuasion. The mastery of this art requires practice, study, and a deep understanding of both the spoken and unspoken elements of effective communication.

A. THE HISTORY OF ORATORY and Its Relevance to the Legal Profession

1. Ancient Origins:

The history of oratory dates back to ancient civilizations, with roots in Greece and Rome. In Greece, prominent figures like Demosthenes and Pericles were celebrated orators known for their persuasive speeches in the Athenian democracy. In Rome, oratory played a significant role in the legal system, with Cicero being one of the most renowned Roman orators and lawyers.

2. Roman Influence:

Roman legal proceedings heavily relied on oratory, as lawyers presented cases and arguments in front of judges and juries. Cicero, a statesman, philosopher, and lawyer, is often considered the epitome of a successful Roman orator. His speeches in the Roman Senate and law courts showcased the power of persuasion and rhetoric.

3. Medieval Europe:

During the medieval period in Europe, oratory continued to be essential, especially within ecclesiastical and legal contexts. The clergy used oratory to deliver sermons, and the legal profession adapted persuasive techniques to present cases in court.

4. Renaissance and Enlightenment:

The Renaissance period witnessed a revival of interest in classical rhetoric and oratory. Influential texts like Aristotle's "Rhetoric" and Cicero's works were rediscovered and studied. The Enlightenment era further emphasized the importance of reason and persuasion in public discourse.

5. American Legal Tradition:

Oratory played a pivotal role in shaping the American legal tradition. Figures like Patrick Henry, known for his "Give me liberty or give me death" speech, and Abraham Lincoln, celebrated for his Gettysburg Address, demonstrated the power of oratory in rallying support and advocating for change.

6. Modern Legal Practice:

In contemporary legal practice, oratory remains highly relevant. Lawyers use persuasive techniques and rhetorical skills to present arguments in court, negotiate settlements, and influence decision-makers. Effective courtroom advocacy often hinges on a lawyer's ability to craft and deliver compelling speeches.

7. Relevance to the Legal Profession:

Oratory is a critical skill for lawyers, as it enables them to:

Present legal arguments convincingly in court, influencing judges and juries.

Advocate for clients, persuading others of the merits of their cases.

Negotiate favorable settlements through persuasive communication.

Effectively communicate complex legal concepts to clients and laypersons.

Build credibility and trust with clients, colleagues, and the public.

The ability to convey legal arguments with clarity and persuasion is a hallmark of a successful legal career. Lawyers who excel in oratory often achieve better outcomes for their clients and make a lasting impact on legal proceedings.

In summary, the history of oratory is deeply intertwined with the legal profession, dating back to ancient civilizations and continuing to be highly relevant in modern legal practice. Oratory is not merely a historical relic; it is a living tradition that shapes the way lawyers present cases, advocate for clients, and engage in the pursuit of justice. Understanding the historical context of oratory helps legal professionals appreciate its enduring importance and its potential to influence legal outcomes.

B. FAMOUS LAWYERS KNOWN for Their Persuasive Speaking Skills

Throughout history, several famous lawyers have earned recognition for their exceptional persuasive speaking skills. These individuals have demonstrated the power of oratory in various contexts, often leaving a lasting impact on legal proceedings, social change, and the course of history. Here are some of the most notable lawyers celebrated for their persuasive speaking abilities:

Abraham Lincoln (1809-1865):

Abraham Lincoln, the 16th President of the United States, was a self-taught lawyer known for his eloquent and persuasive speeches. His Gettysburg Address, delivered during the American Civil War, is a masterpiece of concise and powerful oratory. Lincoln's ability to convey complex ideas with clarity and emotional resonance made him an iconic figure in American history.

Clarence Darrow (1857-1938):

Clarence Darrow, a renowned American lawyer, is often considered one of the greatest trial lawyers in U.S. history. He was known for his passionate and persuasive courtroom speeches, including his defense of John T. Scopes in the Scopes Monkey Trial, where he argued for the teaching of evolution in public schools.

Thurgood Marshall (1908-1993):

Thurgood Marshall was a pioneering lawyer and the first African American Supreme Court Justice. As a civil rights attorney, he delivered persuasive arguments in landmark cases like Brown v. Board of Education, leading to the desegregation of public schools. Marshall's legal advocacy played a pivotal role in advancing civil rights in the United States.

Gerry Spence (1929-present):

Gerry Spence is a contemporary American trial lawyer known for his persuasive speaking skills. He has a remarkable track record of winning high-profile cases and is recognized for his ability to connect with juries on a personal level through compelling storytelling and emotional appeals.

Cicero (106-43 BC):

Cicero, a Roman statesman, philosopher, and lawyer, is celebrated for his masterful oratory. His speeches, including the famous "Pro Milone" and "In Catilinam" orations, demonstrated his exceptional rhetorical skills and played a significant role in the political and legal affairs of ancient Rome.

Mahatma Gandhi (1869-1948):

Mahatma Gandhi, known as the father of the Indian independence movement, was also a trained lawyer. His persuasive communication skills were instrumental in mobilizing nonviolent resistance against British colonial rule in India. His speeches and writings inspired millions and contributed to India's eventual independence.

Barack Obama (1961-present):

Before becoming the 44th President of the United States, Barack Obama was a lawyer and law professor. He is renowned for his powerful and inspirational speeches, including his keynote address at the 2004 Democratic National Convention and his speeches on racial and social issues during his presidency.

Ruth Bader Ginsburg (1933-2020):

The late Ruth Bader Ginsburg, an Associate Justice of the U.S. Supreme Court, was known for her persuasive and meticulously crafted legal opinions. Her written and oral advocacy played a significant role in advancing gender equality and civil rights in the United States.

These lawyers, among others, serve as shining examples of the impact of persuasive speaking skills in the legal profession and beyond. Their ability to articulate ideas, engage audiences, and advocate for justice has left a lasting legacy, shaping legal outcomes and societal change.

C. THE ELEMENTS OF Persuasive Speech for Lawyers: Tone, Cadence, Pacing, and More

In the legal profession, effective persuasion through speech is a fundamental skill. Lawyers use various elements of persuasive speech to present their arguments convincingly, whether in courtrooms, negotiations, or other legal settings. Here are key elements that lawyers utilize to make their speeches persuasive:

Tone:

The tone of speech sets the emotional context of the argument. Lawyers choose their tone carefully to match the message they want to convey. For example, a lawyer may use a confident and authoritative tone when presenting facts, but a compassionate and empathetic tone when discussing sensitive issues.

Cadence:

Cadence refers to the rhythm or flow of speech. Lawyers use variations in cadence to maintain the audience's interest and emphasize key points. Pausing for effect, speeding up or slowing down, and changing the pace can all be effective persuasive techniques.

Pacing:

Pacing involves the speed at which a lawyer speaks. Effective pacing can create emphasis and highlight important information. Lawyers may speak slowly to ensure clarity when explaining complex legal concepts or speed up to build excitement during a compelling argument.

Volume and Intonation:

Lawyers modulate their volume and intonation to convey emotion and emphasize key ideas. Raising one's voice for emphasis, lowering it for seriousness, or using a rising intonation to ask rhetorical questions can all enhance persuasion.

Clarity and Simplicity:

Persuasive speeches are clear and straightforward. Lawyers aim to convey complex legal arguments in simple terms that the audience can understand. Clear and concise language helps build credibility and trust.

Emotional Appeal:

Lawyers often use emotional appeal to connect with their audience. Sharing relatable anecdotes, using empathy, and evoking emotions like sympathy or indignation can make a persuasive argument more compelling.

Credibility and Confidence:

Confidence in speech is persuasive. Lawyers must convey that they believe in the merits of their argument. Confidence in one's voice and body language can inspire trust in the audience.

Rhetorical Devices:

Lawyers employ rhetorical devices like metaphors, analogies, alliteration, and repetition to enhance the impact of their speech. These devices can make arguments more memorable and emotionally resonant.

Non-Verbal Communication:

Non-verbal cues, such as gestures, facial expressions, and body language, play a crucial role in persuasion. Lawyers use these cues to reinforce their spoken words and convey sincerity.

Logical Structure:

A well-structured speech follows a logical progression, with a clear introduction, body, and conclusion. Lawyers use this structure to guide the audience through their arguments and make it easier to follow and accept their points.

Evidentiary Support:

Lawyers bolster their arguments with evidence, citing legal precedents, statutes, facts, and expert opinions. Providing strong evidence enhances the credibility of the speech and strengthens the persuasive appeal.

Rebuttal and Counterarguments:

Addressing opposing viewpoints and counterarguments demonstrates thoroughness and fairness. Lawyers anticipate potential objections and effectively rebut them to strengthen their own position.

Engagement with the Audience:

Lawyers engage with their audience through eye contact, addressing them directly, and using inclusive language. Engaging the audience creates a connection and fosters receptivity to the lawyer's message.

By skillfully incorporating these elements into their speeches, lawyers can enhance their persuasive abilities and effectively advocate for their clients or causes in various legal contexts. Effective persuasion not only influences the outcome of legal proceedings but also contributes to the broader pursuit of justice and legal excellence.

IV. The Power of Persuasion

The power of persuasion refers to the ability to influence, convince, or sway the beliefs, decisions, actions, or opinions of others through effective communication and argumentation. Persuasion is a nuanced art that involves using rhetorical, psychological, and emotional techniques to make a compelling case or appeal to an individual or a group. It relies on the strategic use of words, evidence, logic, and emotional appeals to achieve a desired outcome. The power of persuasion is prevalent in various aspects of life, including sales, marketing, politics, law, and everyday interpersonal interactions. Successful persuasion often results in individuals willingly adopting a particular viewpoint, making a choice, or taking specific actions based on the persuader's convincing arguments or appeals.

A. THE PSYCHOLOGY OF Persuasion and How It Applies to Lawyers

The psychology of persuasion is a field of study that examines the psychological principles and tactics used to influence human behavior, beliefs, decisions, and attitudes. Understanding these principles is crucial for lawyers, as persuasion is a cornerstone of their profession. Here's how the psychology of persuasion applies to lawyers and their practice:

1. Reciprocity:

Application to Lawyers: Lawyers can use the principle of reciprocity by providing valuable information or assistance to potential clients or opposing counsel. This can foster a sense of obligation, making individuals more receptive to the lawyer's message or proposals.

2. Commitment and Consistency:

Application to Lawyers: Lawyers can leverage the desire for consistency by getting individuals to commit to small actions or statements that align with their legal position. Once committed, people tend to remain consistent with their initial commitments, making it easier to persuade them further.

3. Social Proof:

Application to Lawyers: Lawyers can use social proof by showcasing testimonials, case results, or endorsements from satisfied clients or respected colleagues. This demonstrates that others have already trusted the lawyer's services, creating trust and credibility.

4. Authority:

Application to Lawyers: Lawyers can establish their authority by highlighting their expertise, qualifications, and experience in a particular area of law. This can make clients and legal professionals more likely to trust their judgment and advice.

5. Likability:

Application to Lawyers: Building rapport and establishing a likable personality can enhance a lawyer's persuasive abilities. Clients are more likely to be influenced by lawyers they trust and feel comfortable with.

6. Scarcity:

Application to Lawyers: Lawyers can create a sense of urgency or scarcity by highlighting the limited availability of their services or the potential consequences of delaying legal action. This can motivate clients to take action more quickly.

7. Emotional Appeal:

Application to Lawyers: Lawyers often use emotional appeals to connect with jurors, judges, and clients on a personal level. Sharing compelling stories, demonstrating empathy, and appealing to emotions can be highly persuasive in legal arguments.

8. Cognitive Dissonance:

Application to Lawyers: Lawyers can identify and exploit cognitive dissonance in opposing arguments or witnesses' statements. By pointing out inconsistencies, lawyers can weaken the credibility of the opposing side and strengthen their own position.

9. Framing and Priming:

Application to Lawyers: Lawyers can frame their arguments and evidence in a way that primes the decision-maker's mind to view the case from a favorable perspective. Framing can influence how jurors interpret evidence and legal principles.

10. Anchoring:

- Application to Lawyers: Lawyers can use anchoring by presenting an initial offer, settlement, or argument that serves as a reference point for negotiations. This can influence the final outcome by framing subsequent offers and concessions.

11. Psychological Biases:

- Application to Lawyers: Lawyers should be aware of various cognitive biases, such as confirmation bias, hindsight bias, and the availability heuristic, that can affect decision-making. Understanding these biases allows lawyers to present their arguments in ways that mitigate their impact.

By incorporating the principles of persuasion and an understanding of human psychology into their legal practice, lawyers can become more effective advocates for their clients. Persuasive skills are critical in legal proceedings, negotiations, and client interactions, enabling lawyers to achieve favorable outcomes, build trust, and navigate complex legal situations successfully.

B. CASE STUDIES OF Landmark Legal Battles Won Through Persuasive Argumentation

Brown v. Board of Education (1954):

Background: In this landmark case, lawyers argued that racial segregation in public schools violated the Equal Protection Clause of the Fourteenth Amendment.

Persuasive Argumentation: Thurgood Marshall and his legal team used social science evidence, expert testimony, and emotional appeals to convince the Supreme Court that "separate but equal" education was inherently unequal.

Outcome: The Supreme Court ruled unanimously in favor of desegregating public schools, effectively overturning the "separate but equal" doctrine and advancing civil rights in the United States.

Miranda v. Arizona (1966):

Background: In this case, the question was whether Ernesto Miranda's confession to a crime was admissible in court, as he had not been informed of his Fifth Amendment rights.

Persuasive Argumentation: Lawyer John J. Flynn argued that Miranda's confession was obtained without proper warning of his rights, violating the Fifth Amendment's protection against self-incrimination.

Outcome: The Supreme Court ruled in favor of Miranda, establishing the "Miranda warning" requirement for law enforcement, which informs suspects of their rights, including the right to remain silent and the right to an attorney.

Roe v. Wade (1973):

Background: In a landmark case for reproductive rights, lawyers argued that a Texas law criminalizing abortion violated a woman's right to privacy.

Persuasive Argumentation: Attorney Sarah Weddington used a privacy-based argument and emphasized the emotional and physical toll on women due to restrictive abortion laws.

Outcome: The Supreme Court's decision in Roe v. Wade legalized abortion in the United States, recognizing a woman's right to choose within certain limits, based on a persuasive privacy argument.

Obergefell v. Hodges (2015):

Background: This case addressed whether same-sex marriage bans in several states violated the Equal Protection Clause and Due Process Clause of the Fourteenth Amendment.

Persuasive Argumentation: Lawyers argued that denying same-sex couples the right to marry deprived them of essential legal benefits and stigmatized their relationships, thereby violating equal protection and due process rights.

Outcome: The Supreme Court's decision established marriage equality nationwide, allowing same-sex couples to legally marry in all 50 states.

United States v. Microsoft (2001):

Background: In an antitrust case, the U.S. government accused Microsoft of monopolistic practices.

Persuasive Argumentation: Government lawyers argued that Microsoft's actions harmed competition and innovation in the software industry, making a compelling case based on economic analysis and witness testimonies.

Outcome: Microsoft settled the case, agreeing to certain restrictions on its business practices, which reshaped the tech industry and set legal precedents for antitrust enforcement.

These case studies illustrate how persuasive argumentation by skilled lawyers can shape legal outcomes and influence societal change. Effective communication, evidence presentation, and legal reasoning are essential elements in winning landmark legal battles and establishing important legal precedents.

C. ETHICAL CONSIDERATIONS in Using Persuasion in the Courtroom

The use of persuasion in the courtroom is an integral part of legal advocacy, but it must be conducted within ethical boundaries to ensure fairness, justice, and the integrity of the legal system. Lawyers have ethical obligations to both their clients and the legal profession. Here are key ethical considerations when using persuasion in the courtroom:

Candor and Honesty:

Ethical lawyers must be truthful in their arguments, presentations, and interactions with the court, opposing counsel, and witnesses. Deliberate deception or misrepresentation of facts is not permissible.

Respect for Legal Process:

Lawyers should respect the rules and procedures of the legal process. They must not engage in unethical tactics, such as filing frivolous motions or making baseless accusations, to gain an advantage.

Fairness and Impartiality:

Lawyers have an ethical duty to treat all parties, witnesses, and the court with fairness and impartiality. This includes refraining from personal attacks or using discriminatory language.

Duty to the Client vs. Duty to the Court:

Lawyers have a dual role: to represent their clients zealously while also serving as officers of the court. They must balance their duty to advocate for their clients' interests with their duty to uphold the law and promote justice.

Evidence Presentation:

Lawyers must present evidence truthfully and accurately. This includes disclosing evidence that is favorable to the opposing party, as required by the rules of discovery.

Emotional Appeals:

While emotional appeals are often effective in persuasion, lawyers must be cautious when using them. Manipulative or exploitative emotional appeals that unfairly sway jurors or exploit witnesses' vulnerabilities are unethical.

Expert Witnesses:

When presenting expert witnesses, lawyers have an ethical obligation to ensure the experts' testimony is based on reliable and credible scientific or professional knowledge. They should not present false or misleading expert testimony.

Pretrial Public Statements:

Lawyers should refrain from making prejudicial statements to the media or public that could influence potential jurors or undermine a fair trial. Ethical lawyers avoid making comments that could prejudice the case.

Civility and Professionalism:

Lawyers must maintain civility and professionalism in their interactions with opposing counsel. Personal attacks, insults, or unprofessional behavior undermine the ethical standards of the legal profession.

Conflicts of Interest:

Lawyers have a duty to identify and address conflicts of interest promptly. They must avoid situations where their loyalties to multiple clients or personal interests may compromise their ethical obligations.

Client's Best Interests:

While lawyers are obligated to represent their clients' interests vigorously, they should not engage in tactics that are contrary to the client's best interests or that could harm the client in the long run.

Court Orders and Rulings:

Lawyers must abide by court orders and rulings, even if they disagree with them. Challenging court decisions through legal means is acceptable, but violating court orders is unethical.

Confidentiality:

Lawyers must protect client confidentiality and privilege. Sharing confidential information without the client's consent is unethical and can result in disciplinary action.

In summary, ethical considerations are paramount in the use of persuasion in the courtroom. Lawyers have a professional and moral obligation to advocate for their clients effectively while adhering to the ethical principles that underpin the legal profession. Ethical conduct in the courtroom is not only a legal requirement but also essential for maintaining the public's trust and confidence in the legal system.

V. The Voice Beyond the Courtroom

"The Voice Beyond the Courtroom" refers to the influence, impact, and responsibilities of legal professionals outside the traditional boundaries of a courtroom setting. It encompasses the roles lawyers play in society, government, advocacy, and leadership, utilizing their legal expertise, ethical principles, and persuasive abilities to effect positive change and address complex social, political, and ethical issues.

Beyond the courtroom, legal professionals may engage in activities such as policy advocacy, legislative drafting, public speaking, and public service. They leverage their legal knowledge to contribute to the development of laws, regulations, and policies that shape society and impact individuals and communities. This broader influence extends to areas like human rights, civil liberties, social justice, environmental protection, and more.

"The Voice Beyond the Courtroom" emphasizes the multifaceted roles lawyers assume as advocates, advisors, problem solvers, and community leaders. It underscores their capacity to use their legal expertise to make a positive difference in the world by addressing legal, ethical, and societal challenges through various means, including public discourse, writing, education, and community engagement.

A. HOW A LAWYER'S VOICE Influences Negotiations and Settlements

A lawyer's voice is a powerful tool that significantly influences negotiations and settlements in legal matters. Effective communication is a cornerstone of successful negotiation, and a lawyer's voice plays a crucial role in conveying their client's position, building rapport, and ultimately reaching favorable outcomes. Here's how a lawyer's voice influences negotiations and settlements:

Clarity and Articulation: A lawyer's ability to articulate their client's position clearly and concisely is paramount. Clarity in communication helps all parties involved understand the issues, options, and potential solutions, reducing misunderstandings and misinterpretations.

Confidence and Authority: A lawyer who speaks confidently and authoritatively can instill confidence in their client's position and negotiation strategy. This can influence the opposing party to take their arguments and proposals more seriously.

Emotional Tone: The tone and emotional expression in a lawyer's voice can set the mood for negotiations. Empathy, understanding, and a calm demeanor can foster a cooperative atmosphere, making it more likely for parties to find common ground.

Active Listening: Effective negotiation requires not only speaking but also active listening. A lawyer's voice reflects their attentiveness to the concerns and interests of the opposing party, which can help build trust and facilitate compromise.

Persuasive Techniques: Lawyers use persuasive language and rhetorical devices to advocate for their client's position. These techniques, when skillfully employed, can sway the opinions and decisions of the opposing party or mediator.

Negotiation Style: A lawyer's voice can reflect their negotiation style, which may be assertive, cooperative, or a combination of both. The choice of style can impact the tone of negotiations and the likelihood of reaching an agreement.

Conflict Resolution: When conflicts arise during negotiations, a lawyer's voice can be instrumental in de-escalating tensions. Calm and respectful communication can prevent disputes from escalating and facilitate compromise.

Building Rapport: Establishing rapport and a positive working relationship with opposing counsel or parties is essential. A lawyer's voice can convey respect, professionalism, and a willingness to collaborate, which can lead to smoother negotiations.

Effective Questioning: Lawyers use questioning techniques to elicit information, clarify positions, and uncover underlying interests. The tone and phrasing of questions can influence the quality and depth of responses from the opposing party.

Final Settlement Terms: In the final stages of negotiations, a lawyer's voice plays a role in articulating and confirming settlement terms. The clarity and precision of this communication are crucial to ensure all parties are in agreement.

Mediation and Arbitration: In alternative dispute resolution processes like mediation and arbitration, a lawyer's voice is central to presenting their client's case effectively to the neutral third party. Persuasive advocacy can lead to favorable outcomes.

Drafting Settlement Agreements: After negotiations, lawyers use their voice in the drafting of settlement agreements. Clear and comprehensive language is essential to avoid future disputes regarding the terms of the settlement.

In summary, a lawyer's voice is a multifaceted tool that influences negotiations and settlements through effective communication, persuasion, and professionalism. It plays a pivotal role in creating an environment conducive to compromise, resolution, and the achievement of the client's goals. A skilled lawyer recognizes the importance of their voice and employs it strategically to secure favorable outcomes for their clients.

B. The Role of a Lawyer's Voice in Public Speaking Engagements and Media Appearances

A lawyer's voice is a critical asset when they engage in public speaking engagements and media appearances. Effective communication is key in these contexts, as lawyers often serve as spokespersons, advocates, or commentators on legal, social, or policy issues. Here's how a lawyer's voice plays a crucial role in these settings:

Credibility and Authority: A lawyer's voice conveys credibility and authority, establishing them as experts in their field. A confident and well-modulated voice enhances the audience's trust in the lawyer's knowledge and insights.

Clarity and Persuasion: Clear and persuasive communication is essential in public speaking and media appearances. A lawyer's voice helps them articulate complex legal concepts or arguments in a way that is understandable and compelling to a broad audience.

Emotional Connection: The tone and emotional expression in a lawyer's voice can connect with the audience on a personal level. Expressing empathy, concern, or passion when discussing legal issues can resonate with viewers or listeners and make the message more impactful.

Effective Storytelling: Lawyers often use their voice to tell stories that illustrate legal principles or humanize complex cases. Storytelling engages the audience and helps them relate to the legal issues at hand.

Debates and Discussions: In panel discussions, debates, or interviews, a lawyer's voice influences their ability to present arguments persuasively and engage in meaningful exchanges with others. A well-modulated voice can command attention and foster productive dialogue.

Public Advocacy: Lawyers may use their voice to advocate for specific causes or policy changes in the public arena. An impassioned and persuasive voice can rally support and mobilize action on important social or legal issues.

Effective Messaging: Lawyers use their voice to deliver key messages effectively, ensuring that the audience takes away the intended points. This is crucial when addressing legal matters in the media or public forums.

Media Training: Lawyers often undergo media training to enhance their speaking skills. This training helps them control nervousness, handle difficult questions, and convey their message clearly and concisely through their voice.

Interview Preparedness: Lawyers need to be prepared for media interviews, where their voice is front and center. They must anticipate questions, craft responses, and practice their speaking delivery to ensure they come across as well-informed and confident.

Online Presence: In an increasingly digital world, lawyers engage in podcasts, webinars, and social media platforms. Their voice, whether spoken or written, plays a crucial role in building an online presence and engaging with virtual audiences.

Advocacy for Clients: In high-profile cases, lawyers may use media appearances to advocate for their clients and shape public opinion. Their voice in these instances can influence public perception and, indirectly, legal outcomes.

Educational Outreach: Lawyers use their voice to educate the public about legal rights, responsibilities, and the justice system. They may participate in community events, legal clinics, or educational programs to inform and empower others.

In summary, a lawyer's voice is a versatile tool that helps them effectively communicate, persuade, and advocate in public speaking engagements and media appearances. Whether addressing a courtroom, a television audience, or an online platform, a lawyer's voice is instrumental in conveying their expertise, influencing opinions, and advancing their goals and causes.

C. BUILDING A PERSONAL Brand Through Effective Communication

Building a personal brand as a lawyer involves establishing a distinct professional identity, reputation, and image. Effective communication plays a central role in shaping and promoting that brand. Here's how lawyers can build a personal brand through effective communication:

Clarity of Message: Articulate a clear and concise message that defines who you are as a lawyer, what you stand for, and what unique value you offer to clients or the legal profession. Make sure your message is easily understood by your target audience.

Consistent Branding: Maintain consistency in your communication across various platforms, including your website, social media, professional profiles, and in-person interactions. Consistency reinforces your brand identity and helps people recognize and remember you.

Authenticity: Authenticity is crucial in building trust. Be genuine and transparent in your communication. Share your values, beliefs, and experiences that align with your brand. Authenticity helps you connect with your audience on a personal level.

Professionalism: Uphold high standards of professionalism in all your communication, whether it's in legal documents, emails, public speaking, or interactions with clients and colleagues. Professionalism is a key element of a strong personal brand.

Engagement: Actively engage with your audience through various channels. Respond to comments, questions, and feedback promptly and thoughtfully. Engagement builds a sense of community and fosters loyalty among your followers.

Content Creation: Create valuable and relevant content that showcases your expertise. Write articles, blog posts, or whitepapers on legal topics of interest. Share insights, opinions, and case studies that demonstrate your knowledge.

Public Speaking: Participate in public speaking engagements, conferences, or webinars to showcase your expertise. Effective speaking skills can enhance your credibility and visibility in your practice area.

Networking: Build relationships with colleagues, mentors, and peers in the legal community. Effective networking involves active listening, asking questions, and contributing meaningfully to conversations.

Use of Social Media: Leverage social media platforms to connect with a broader audience. Share legal updates, engage in discussions, and demonstrate your thought leadership in your chosen field.

Professional Development: Communicate your commitment to professional development and staying updated on legal developments. This reinforces your dedication to excellence and positions you as a trusted resource.

Client Testimonials: Encourage satisfied clients to provide testimonials and reviews. Positive client feedback is a powerful form of communication that bolsters your reputation and credibility.

Mentorship and Giving Back: Showcase your commitment to mentorship, pro bono work, or community service. These activities reflect positively on your personal brand by highlighting your dedication to making a positive impact.

Effective Personal Branding Statement: Craft a personal branding statement that encapsulates your identity as a lawyer. Use this statement in your online profiles, bios, and marketing materials to create a strong first impression.

Professional Appearance: Your visual communication, including attire and professional photos, should align with your brand. Ensure that your appearance reinforces the image you want to project.

Continuous Learning: Demonstrate your commitment to professional growth by pursuing continuing legal education and certifications. Highlight these achievements in your communication to reinforce your expertise.

Building a personal brand through effective communication is an ongoing process. It requires self-awareness, consistency, and a dedication to aligning your actions and messages with your desired brand identity. Over time, a well-crafted personal brand can enhance your reputation, attract clients, and open up opportunities for career advancement in the legal profession.

VI. Overcoming Challenges

"Overcoming challenges" refers to the process of successfully facing and navigating through difficult or adverse circumstances, obstacles, problems, or adversities in life. It involves developing strategies, resilience, and determination to address and conquer these challenges, ultimately achieving personal growth, positive outcomes, or desired goals.

Overcoming challenges is not merely about surmounting obstacles but also about learning from the experiences, adapting to changing circumstances, and building the capacity to handle future challenges. It often requires a combination of mental and emotional strength, problem-solving skills, perseverance, and a willingness to seek support or resources when necessary.

Individuals, organizations, and societies encounter a wide range of challenges, including personal hardships, professional setbacks, health issues, financial difficulties, societal issues, and global crises. The ability to overcome these challenges is a testament to human resilience and the capacity to thrive in the face of adversity. It is a fundamental aspect of personal development, resilience-building, and achieving long-term success and well-being.

A. COMMON CHALLENGES Lawyers Face in Developing Their Voices

Developing and honing one's voice as a lawyer is a multifaceted process that involves various challenges. Lawyers often encounter obstacles that can affect their ability to communicate effectively, build their professional brand, and advocate for their clients. Here are some common challenges lawyers face in developing their voices:

Lack of Confidence: Some lawyers may struggle with self-doubt and a lack of confidence when speaking in legal settings. This can hinder their ability to assert themselves and present their arguments persuasively.

Legal Jargon: The legal profession is known for its complex terminology and jargon. Lawyers must navigate the challenge of communicating legal concepts in a way that is understandable to clients, judges, jurors, and the general public.

Nervousness in Public Speaking: Public speaking is a significant part of a lawyer's role, whether in courtrooms, boardrooms, or public forums. Many lawyers face anxiety and nervousness when speaking in front of others, which can impact their delivery and effectiveness.

Adaptability: Lawyers often need to adapt their communication style to various audiences, from clients with different backgrounds to judges with distinct preferences. Adapting to these diverse audiences can be challenging.

Time Constraints: Lawyers frequently work under tight time constraints, requiring them to convey complex information quickly and efficiently. This pressure can affect the clarity and effectiveness of their communication.

Balancing Legal and Client Needs: Lawyers must balance the need to communicate legal advice and strategies with the need to address their clients' emotional concerns and expectations. Striking this balance can be challenging.

Negotiation Tensions: Negotiating settlements and agreements can be emotionally charged. Lawyers need to manage their emotions and maintain professionalism while advocating for their clients' interests.

Staying Informed: The legal field is dynamic, with laws and regulations constantly evolving. Lawyers must stay informed about changes in their practice areas and effectively communicate these changes to clients.

Handling Difficult Conversations: Lawyers often find themselves in challenging conversations, such as delivering unfavorable legal advice or discussing sensitive topics with clients. Managing these conversations while maintaining trust can be a challenge.

Ethical Considerations: Lawyers must navigate ethical considerations, such as client confidentiality and honesty, in their communication. Balancing ethical obligations with effective advocacy can be complex.

Building a Personal Brand: Developing a distinct professional identity and personal brand can be challenging, as it requires clear and consistent communication that aligns with one's values and goals.

Handling High-Stakes Cases: Lawyers involved in high-stakes cases may face intense pressure and scrutiny, which can impact their ability to communicate effectively and confidently.

Staying Current with Technology: As technology plays an increasing role in the legal profession, lawyers must adapt to new communication tools and platforms, such as digital legal research and virtual court proceedings.

Overcoming these challenges and developing a strong and effective voice as a lawyer often requires a combination of training, practice, mentorship, and self-awareness. Additionally, seeking support from colleagues, communication coaches, or professional development programs can be instrumental in addressing these challenges and honing one's skills in the legal profession.

B. Strategies for Improving Vocal Confidence and Clarity

Improving vocal confidence and clarity is essential for lawyers to effectively communicate and advocate for their clients. Here are some strategies that can help lawyers enhance their vocal skills:

Voice Coaching: Consider working with a voice coach or speech therapist who specializes in vocal training. They can provide personalized guidance, exercises, and feedback to improve vocal confidence, clarity, and projection.

Practice and Rehearsal: Practice is key to building vocal confidence. Rehearse speeches, presentations, and arguments multiple times before delivering them in a formal setting. Record yourself and analyze the recordings for areas of improvement.

Breathing Exercises: Proper breathing is fundamental to vocal clarity and projection. Practice deep breathing exercises to strengthen your diaphragm and improve breath control. Breathing exercises can also help reduce nervousness.

Articulation Exercises: Engage in articulation exercises to improve the clarity of your speech. Practice enunciating words and consonants clearly to avoid mumbling or slurring.

Pitch and Tone Control: Experiment with varying your pitch and tone to add emphasis and variety to your speech. A monotone voice can lead to disengagement, while modulation can keep your audience's attention.

Slow Down: Speaking too quickly can lead to unclear speech. Practice speaking at a moderate pace to ensure that your words are enunciated clearly and your audience has time to absorb information.

Record and Self-Assess: Record your speeches or courtroom presentations and listen to them critically. Identify areas where you can improve your vocal clarity, confidence, and tone.

Visualization: Before speaking engagements, visualize yourself speaking confidently and clearly. Positive visualization can help reduce anxiety and boost self-assurance.

Feedback and Peer Review: Seek feedback from colleagues or mentors who can provide constructive criticism and suggestions for improvement. Peer review can offer valuable insights into your vocal performance.

Public Speaking Courses: Consider enrolling in public speaking or communication courses. These courses often include exercises and techniques to enhance vocal clarity and confidence.

Body Language: Be mindful of your body language, as it complements your vocal communication. Maintain good posture, make eye contact, and use gestures appropriately to reinforce your message.

Reduce Vocal Stress: Prioritize vocal health by staying hydrated, avoiding excessive caffeine and alcohol, and getting adequate rest. Vocal stress can lead to hoarseness and reduced clarity.

Visualization: Visualize success and confidence before important speaking engagements. This mental preparation can boost your vocal confidence.

Join Toastmasters: Consider joining a Toastmasters club, where you can practice public speaking, receive feedback, and develop your vocal skills in a supportive environment.

Recorded Mock Trials: For lawyers involved in litigation, conducting mock trials with recordings can help you refine your courtroom presence, including vocal delivery.

Remember that improving vocal confidence and clarity is an ongoing process. Consistent practice and a commitment to self-improvement are key to enhancing your vocal skills as a lawyer. Over time, these efforts will not only boost your effectiveness in legal settings but also enhance your overall communication abilities.

C. BALANCING ASSERTIVENESS with Professionalism

Balancing assertiveness with professionalism is a critical skill for lawyers. While it's important to advocate vigorously for clients and present persuasive arguments, it must be done within the bounds of professional ethics and decorum. Here are strategies for striking this balance effectively:

Know Your Audience: Tailor your communication style to your audience. A more assertive approach may be appropriate in court or during negotiations, while a more collaborative tone might be better for discussions with colleagues or clients.

Preparation: Thoroughly prepare for all interactions. When you are well-prepared, you can speak confidently and assertively, knowing that your arguments are well-founded.

Active Listening: Effective communication includes active listening. Take the time to listen carefully to opposing arguments and concerns. Acknowledge valid points and address them professionally.

Respectful Language: Use respectful and non-inflammatory language, even when challenging opposing arguments. Avoid personal attacks, insults, or derogatory remarks.

Maintain Composure: Maintain emotional control, especially in contentious situations. Losing your temper or becoming overly aggressive can harm your professional reputation.

Professional Disagreements: In disagreements with colleagues or opposing counsel, focus on the merits of the argument rather than making it personal. Professionalism requires addressing the issues at hand, not attacking individuals.

Civility: Uphold civility and decorum in all professional interactions. Be polite, courteous, and respectful, even when differences of opinion arise.

Ethical Considerations: Always adhere to ethical guidelines and rules of professional conduct. Ethical violations can damage your reputation and career.

Use of Evidence: Rely on facts, evidence, and the law to support your assertions. Present a strong case rather than relying solely on assertiveness.

Client Communication: When communicating with clients, explain the potential outcomes of various legal strategies clearly and honestly. Maintain open and transparent communication to manage expectations.

Negotiation Skills: In negotiation, strike a balance between assertiveness and collaboration. Advocate for your client's interests while seeking common ground and potential solutions.

Conflict Resolution: Develop conflict resolution skills to address disputes professionally and constructively. Mediation or alternative dispute resolution methods can be effective in resolving conflicts while preserving relationships.

Mentorship: Seek mentorship or guidance from experienced lawyers who can provide insights on balancing assertiveness and professionalism. Learn from their experiences and observe their approach to advocacy.

Self-Reflection: Regularly assess your communication style and its impact on others. Are you coming across as assertive without being overly aggressive? Self-reflection can lead to self-improvement.

Role Modeling: Be a role model for professionalism in your legal community. Your behavior can set the standard for others in the field.

Continuing Education: Stay informed about changes in legal ethics, communication best practices, and professional conduct through continuing legal education.

Balancing assertiveness with professionalism is essential for maintaining credibility, fostering trust, and achieving positive outcomes in legal practice. By navigating disputes and interactions with a measured and respectful approach, lawyers can build strong professional relationships, uphold ethical standards, and effectively advocate for their clients.

VII. The Changing Landscape of Legal Advocacy

"The Changing Landscape of Legal Advocacy" refers to the evolving and dynamic nature of the legal profession, encompassing shifts in strategies, tools, and approaches employed by lawyers to advocate for their clients and causes. This concept reflects the recognition that legal advocacy is influenced by a range of factors, including technological advancements, societal changes, legal reforms, and shifts in public perception.

Key elements of the changing landscape of legal advocacy include:

Technological Advancements: The integration of technology in legal practice has transformed how lawyers research, analyze, and present cases. E-discovery tools, legal research software, and virtual court proceedings are examples of technological changes impacting advocacy.

Access to Information: The internet and digital platforms have democratized access to legal information, empowering individuals to better understand their rights and legal options. This has altered the dynamics of client-lawyer relationships.

Alternative Dispute Resolution: The growth of alternative dispute resolution methods, such as mediation and arbitration, has provided new avenues for resolving legal conflicts outside traditional court settings. Lawyers now often employ these approaches to achieve more efficient and client-centric outcomes.

Diversity and Inclusion: Legal advocacy increasingly recognizes the importance of diversity and inclusion, both within the legal profession and in the representation of clients. A more diverse legal workforce brings varied perspectives and approaches to advocacy.

Social Justice Movements: Advocacy has been influenced by societal movements addressing issues like racial justice, gender equality, and environmental protection. Lawyers are increasingly engaged in advocacy aligned with these causes.

Globalization: The interconnectedness of the global economy and legal systems has expanded the scope of legal advocacy, with lawyers often working on cross-border issues and collaborating internationally.

Public Engagement: Lawyers are leveraging social media and digital platforms to engage with the public, disseminate legal information, and advocate for causes. This has expanded the reach of legal advocacy beyond traditional audiences.

Environmental and Technological Challenges: Legal advocacy is adapting to address emerging challenges, such as climate change, cybersecurity, and data privacy, which require specialized expertise and strategies.

Legal Reforms: Changes in legislation and regulatory frameworks continually shape the practice of law and advocacy. Lawyers must adapt to these reforms and advocate for changes when necessary.

Ethical Considerations: The evolving landscape also includes ethical considerations, such as client confidentiality in the digital age, professional responsibility in online communication, and ethical implications of emerging technologies.

"The Changing Landscape of Legal Advocacy" underscores the need for lawyers to adapt, innovate, and remain attuned to developments in law, technology, society, and ethics. Successful legal advocates must navigate these changes while upholding the core principles of justice, fairness, and the rule of law, ultimately serving the best interests of their clients and the broader public.

A. How Technology and Remote Work Impact a Lawyer's Voice

Technology and remote work have transformed the way lawyers practice and communicate, including the way they use their voices. Here's how these changes impact a lawyer's voice:

Virtual Communication: Remote work and virtual meetings are now common in the legal profession. Lawyers often communicate via video conferences and teleconferences, which require adjustments in vocal tone, clarity, and engagement. Lawyers need to convey authority and professionalism effectively through a screen.

Voice Fatigue: Extended virtual meetings, especially those involving negotiations or court proceedings, can lead to voice fatigue. Lawyers may need to speak for extended periods without the physical presence cues that come with in-person interactions.

Technology Tools: Lawyers use various voice-related technology tools, such as voice recognition software and digital transcription services, to streamline their work. Familiarity with and effective use of these tools can impact voice efficiency.

Multimodal Communication: Lawyers often communicate through written messages, emails, and chat platforms alongside verbal communication. Balancing effective written and spoken communication is essential for clarity and professionalism.

Digital Recordings: Court hearings and depositions are increasingly recorded digitally. Lawyers need to ensure that their spoken words are recorded accurately, which can impact subsequent legal proceedings.

Client Consultations: Remote consultations with clients may require lawyers to adapt their communication style to ensure that clients understand legal matters without the benefit of face-to-face interactions.

Stress and Isolation: Remote work can lead to feelings of stress and isolation. These emotional states can affect vocal quality and engagement during virtual interactions.

Audio Quality: Technical issues such as poor audio quality, background noise, and disruptions can affect the effectiveness of remote communication. Lawyers need to manage these challenges to maintain professional voice quality.

Virtual Court Proceedings: The rise of virtual court proceedings can change the dynamics of courtroom advocacy. Lawyers must learn to project their voices effectively and use technology to present their cases persuasively.

Training and Adaptation: Lawyers may need training in virtual communication and voice management for remote work environments. This includes techniques for projecting their voices, managing stress, and maintaining vocal health.

Client Expectations: Clients may have different expectations for virtual interactions compared to in-person meetings. Lawyers must be attuned to these expectations and adapt their vocal style accordingly.

Hybrid Work Models: Some law firms are adopting hybrid work models that combine remote and in-office work. Lawyers must adapt to shifting environments and potentially different communication norms.

In summary, technology and remote work have introduced new challenges and opportunities for lawyers to manage their voices effectively. Adaptation, training, and a conscious effort to maintain vocal health and professionalism in virtual settings are crucial for success in the evolving landscape of legal communication.

B. THE ROLE OF DIVERSITY and Inclusion in the Legal Profession and Its Impact on Voices

Diversity and inclusion play a pivotal role in the legal profession and significantly impact how lawyers use their voices. Here's an exploration of their roles and influence:

Diverse Perspectives: Diversity in the legal profession brings together individuals from various backgrounds, cultures, and experiences. This diversity of perspectives enriches discussions and debates, allowing for a broader range of voices to be heard.

Representation: A diverse legal profession ensures that the voices and interests of different communities and demographics are represented. Lawyers from underrepresented groups can advocate for issues that may not receive attention otherwise.

Inclusive Advocacy: Lawyers practicing in diverse and inclusive environments are better equipped to advocate for clients with diverse backgrounds. They can empathize with their clients' experiences and effectively communicate their needs and concerns.

Cultural Competency: Lawyers working in diverse teams or with diverse clients often develop cultural competency, which includes understanding the nuances of communication and language within various communities. This competency enhances their ability to communicate effectively.

Empathy and Understanding: Inclusion fosters empathy and understanding among legal professionals. Lawyers are more likely to listen actively to their colleagues and clients, considering their unique perspectives and experiences.

Reducing Bias: Diverse and inclusive legal environments promote fairness and reduce biases. Lawyers are more likely to challenge discriminatory practices and stereotypes, leading to more equitable legal outcomes.

Client Trust: Clients from diverse backgrounds may feel more comfortable working with lawyers who understand their cultural or social contexts. This trust can lead to more open and effective communication.

Mentorship and Leadership: Diverse voices in leadership positions can serve as role models and mentors for aspiring lawyers from underrepresented groups, encouraging their participation and influence in the legal profession.

Educational Initiatives: Law schools and legal organizations are increasingly incorporating diversity and inclusion into their curricula and programs. This education helps lawyers develop a broader perspective on legal issues and communication.

Public Perception: The legal profession's commitment to diversity and inclusion can influence public perception. Clients and the public may be more inclined to trust and engage with a legal system that reflects the diversity of the community it serves.

Advocacy for Inclusive Policies: Lawyers with diverse backgrounds often advocate for policies that promote diversity, equity, and inclusion within law firms, legal organizations, and the broader legal community.

Professional Networks: Diverse legal associations and affinity groups provide spaces for lawyers to network, share experiences, and collectively advocate for change. These networks can amplify the voices of underrepresented groups.

Legal Advocacy for Equity: Lawyers often engage in legal advocacy to address issues related to discrimination, bias, and social justice. Their voices can be powerful tools for advancing equity and inclusivity in society.

In conclusion, diversity and inclusion are essential components of a vibrant and just legal profession. They bring forth a variety of voices, perspectives, and experiences that enrich legal discourse, enhance advocacy, and contribute to a more equitable and effective legal system. Embracing diversity and inclusion not only benefits the legal profession but also has far-reaching implications for the broader society it serves.

C. ADAPTING TO EVOLVING Communication Platforms

In the ever-changing landscape of the legal profession, lawyers must adapt to evolving communication platforms to effectively advocate for their clients and stay relevant. Here are key considerations for lawyers as they navigate new communication tools and platforms:

Digital Legal Research: Embrace digital legal research tools and platforms to streamline the process of finding and analyzing legal precedents, statutes, and case law. Online databases and legal research software offer efficient ways to access information.

E-Filing and Court Technology: Familiarize yourself with e-filing systems and other court technologies. Many courts now require electronic filing of documents, and virtual court proceedings have become more common.

Virtual Meetings and Depositions: Develop proficiency in conducting virtual meetings, depositions, and hearings. Platforms like Zoom and Microsoft Teams have become integral for remote communication in the legal field.

Secure Communication: Prioritize secure communication methods to protect client confidentiality and sensitive information. Encrypted email services and secure messaging apps are essential for maintaining privacy.

Online Collaboration: Leverage online collaboration tools like Google Workspace and Microsoft 365 to work seamlessly with colleagues and clients, whether you are in the office or working remotely.

Digital Document Management: Implement digital document management systems to organize, store, and retrieve legal documents and case files efficiently. This reduces reliance on physical paperwork.

Client Portals: Use client portals to securely share documents, updates, and communications with clients. These portals provide a centralized location for clients to access their case information.

Social Media Engagement: Engage strategically on social media platforms to build your professional brand and network with colleagues and potential clients. Maintain professionalism and adhere to ethical guidelines in online interactions.

Content Creation: Consider creating legal content, such as blogs, podcasts, or webinars, to showcase your expertise and engage with a broader audience online. Content can also serve as a valuable resource for clients and prospects.

Data Privacy Compliance: Stay informed about data privacy regulations and compliance requirements, especially when handling personal or sensitive information. Ensure that your communication platforms meet data protection standards.

Cybersecurity Awareness: Develop cybersecurity awareness to protect yourself and your clients from cyber threats. Regularly update your knowledge of cybersecurity best practices and implement them in your communication practices.

Virtual Networking: Participate in virtual networking events, webinars, and conferences to stay connected with colleagues, clients, and industry developments.

Legal Tech Adoption: Explore legal technology solutions that can automate routine tasks, enhance efficiency, and improve client service. Legal tech tools can help you adapt to new communication platforms more effectively.

Continuing Education: Invest in continuing legal education that focuses on technology and communication trends in the legal field. Staying informed about industry developments is crucial.

Feedback and Evaluation: Solicit feedback from clients and colleagues about your communication methods and adapt based on their preferences and needs.

Adapting to evolving communication platforms is not only a necessity in the modern legal profession but also an opportunity to enhance client service, streamline workflows, and stay competitive. By remaining open to new technologies and communication strategies, lawyers can effectively advocate for their clients while also improving their own efficiency and effectiveness.

VIII. The Future of Legal Advocacy

"The Future of Legal Advocacy" refers to the evolving landscape of legal practice and the anticipated changes, trends, and innovations that will shape how lawyers advocate for their clients and advance legal causes in the coming years. This concept encompasses a range of developments, including technological advancements, shifts in legal procedures, changes in societal expectations, and emerging challenges and opportunities in the legal profession.

Key elements of the future of legal advocacy include:

Technological Advancements: The integration of artificial intelligence, data analytics, automation, and blockchain technology is expected to transform legal research, document review, contract analysis, and other aspects of legal practice.

Virtual Courts and Remote Proceedings: The adoption of virtual courtrooms, online dispute resolution, and remote legal proceedings will continue to grow, impacting how lawyers represent clients and interact with the legal system.

Access to Legal Services: Innovations in legal technology and alternative service providers are expected to increase access to legal services, potentially changing the role of traditional law firms and lawyers.

Ethical and Regulatory Changes: Evolving ethical and regulatory considerations will accompany the use of emerging technologies, requiring lawyers to navigate new rules governing their professional conduct.

Data Privacy and Cybersecurity: Lawyers will need to address increasingly complex data privacy and cybersecurity challenges, both in their own practices and in advising clients on compliance and risk mitigation.

Environmental and Social Justice: Legal advocacy will play a pivotal role in addressing pressing issues such as climate change, social justice, and human rights, requiring lawyers to adapt their strategies and priorities.

Client-Centric Approaches: Legal services are expected to become more client-centric, with a focus on personalized, transparent, and accessible legal representation.

Collaborative and Multidisciplinary Models: Collaborative and multidisciplinary approaches to legal problem-solving, involving lawyers, technologists, data analysts, and other professionals, will gain prominence.

Globalization and Cross-Border Legal Issues: Lawyers will increasingly engage in cross-border legal matters, necessitating familiarity with international law, treaties, and regulations.

Continuing Legal Education: Lifelong learning and continuing legal education will be crucial for lawyers to stay abreast of evolving legal landscapes and technologies.

Diversity, Equity, and Inclusion: The legal profession's commitment to diversity, equity, and inclusion will continue to grow, impacting the composition of the legal workforce and the focus of legal advocacy.

Legal Tech Integration: Lawyers will need to integrate legal tech tools seamlessly into their practice to enhance efficiency, reduce costs, and deliver better outcomes for clients.

Legal AI and Predictive Analytics: Artificial intelligence and predictive analytics will assist lawyers in legal research, case prediction, contract analysis, and risk assessment.

Environmental Sustainability: Sustainable and environmentally conscious legal practices will align with growing concerns about the ecological impact of legal processes and proceedings.

"The Future of Legal Advocacy" underscores the need for lawyers to be proactive, adaptable, and forward-thinking in navigating the changing legal landscape. Embracing technology, addressing ethical and regulatory challenges, and advocating for justice and equity will be essential components of legal advocacy in the future. Ultimately, the future of legal advocacy holds opportunities for innovation, increased access to justice, and the potential to address complex global challenges through the legal profession.

A. SPECULATIONS ON the Future of Legal Practice and Communication

The future of legal practice and communication is likely to be shaped by several evolving trends and innovations. While these speculations are not exhaustive, they provide insight into the potential directions that the legal profession may take:

Increased Automation: Legal research, contract analysis, and document review are likely to be heavily automated, reducing the time spent on routine tasks. Lawyers may become more focused on strategic thinking, negotiation, and client counseling.

AI-Powered Legal Assistants: Virtual legal assistants, powered by artificial intelligence, may assist lawyers in managing their caseloads, scheduling, and client interactions. These AI-powered assistants can provide quick access to legal information and analysis.

Virtual Reality (VR) Courtrooms: The use of virtual reality technology could revolutionize court proceedings. Lawyers and judges may participate in virtual courtrooms from remote locations, enhancing access to justice.

Blockchain for Legal Transactions: Blockchain technology may be widely adopted for secure legal transactions, such as property transfers, intellectual property rights management, and smart contracts. Lawyers may need to adapt to this technology.

Advanced Legal Analytics: Predictive analytics and data-driven insights could help lawyers anticipate legal outcomes, assess risks, and make more informed decisions for clients.

Remote Jury Selection and Trials: Jury selection and trials may occur remotely, allowing lawyers to connect with jurors and present evidence virtually. This could lead to changes in trial strategies and advocacy techniques.

Online Dispute Resolution (ODR): ODR platforms and algorithms may facilitate the resolution of disputes outside traditional courts, impacting how lawyers represent clients in negotiation and mediation processes.

Global Law Firms: The globalization of legal services may lead to the emergence of multinational law firms that navigate complex international legal landscapes. Lawyers will need to be well-versed in international law and regulations.

Voice and Chatbot Legal Assistants: Voice-activated legal assistants and chatbots could assist lawyers in drafting legal documents, answering common legal questions, and providing legal information to clients.

Enhanced Cybersecurity: Lawyers will need to stay vigilant against evolving cyber threats and data breaches, implementing robust cybersecurity measures to protect client information.

Remote and Flexible Work Models: Remote work and flexible work arrangements may become more common, requiring lawyers to adapt to virtual law practices and manage client relationships from various locations.

Sustainable Legal Practices: Environmental sustainability may become a consideration in legal practice, with lawyers adopting eco-friendly approaches to legal processes and procedures.

Continuing Legal Education in Technology: Lifelong learning in legal technology and digital literacy will be essential for lawyers to remain competitive and relevant in the evolving legal landscape.

AI-Powered Legal Research Tools: Advanced AI tools may assist lawyers in legal research by providing tailored legal information, case summaries, and relevant precedents quickly.

Personalized Legal Services: Client-centric legal services may become the norm, with lawyers offering customized solutions, transparent fee structures, and accessible communication channels to meet clients' specific needs.

These speculations suggest that the legal profession will continue to evolve rapidly, driven by technological advancements, changes in client expectations, and global dynamics. Lawyers who adapt to these developments, embrace innovation, and prioritize effective communication will be well-positioned for success in the future of legal practice.

B. PREDICTIONS FOR How Artificial Intelligence and Other Technologies May Change the Game in Legal Practice and Communication:

Legal Research Augmentation: Artificial intelligence will further enhance legal research by providing lawyers with quick access to comprehensive databases, predictive analytics, and customized case law analysis. AI-powered research tools will save time, improve accuracy, and enable lawyers to focus on more strategic aspects of their cases.

Contract Review Automation: AI-driven contract analysis tools will become integral to legal practice, automating the review of contracts, identifying potential risks, and suggesting revisions. This will streamline contract negotiation and drafting.

Predictive Analytics for Case Outcomes: Lawyers will rely on predictive analytics models to assess the likelihood of case outcomes, helping them make data-driven decisions, manage client expectations, and develop more effective legal strategies.

Chatbots and Virtual Legal Assistants: Chatbots and virtual assistants will handle routine client inquiries, schedule appointments, and provide preliminary legal information. This will improve client engagement and free up lawyers for more complex tasks.

Natural Language Processing (NLP): NLP technologies will enable lawyers to extract insights from vast amounts of unstructured data, such as legal documents and transcripts. This will aid in case analysis, legal research, and evidence discovery.

Virtual Reality Courtrooms: Virtual reality will offer immersive courtroom experiences, allowing lawyers to present evidence and arguments in a more engaging and persuasive manner. VR courtrooms may also facilitate remote trial participation.

Blockchain for Legal Transactions: Blockchain technology will be used for secure and transparent legal transactions, including property transfers, intellectual property rights management, and notarization of documents. Smart contracts will automate contract execution.

Ethical AI and Bias Mitigation: As AI becomes more prominent, addressing ethical concerns and mitigating bias in algorithms will be a priority. Lawyers will need to ensure that AI tools adhere to ethical guidelines and promote fairness.

Client-Centric Platforms: Client portals and mobile apps will provide clients with real-time updates on case progress, invoices, and legal documents. These platforms will enhance client satisfaction and transparency.

Online Dispute Resolution (ODR): ODR platforms will simplify dispute resolution by providing accessible and efficient online mechanisms for settling legal disputes. Lawyers will adapt their negotiation and advocacy strategies to this changing landscape.

Data Privacy and Cybersecurity Tools: Lawyers will utilize advanced tools to protect client data and navigate evolving data privacy regulations. AI-powered cybersecurity solutions will help identify and respond to threats proactively.

Multidisciplinary Legal Teams: Law firms will assemble multidisciplinary teams, including lawyers, data scientists, technologists, and industry experts, to address complex legal challenges effectively.

Remote Collaboration and Court Proceedings: Remote work and virtual court proceedings will continue to evolve, requiring lawyers to excel in virtual communication, digital document management, and online advocacy.

Global Legal Services: Globalization will lead to more cross-border legal work. Lawyers will need to navigate international regulations, understand diverse legal systems, and communicate effectively across cultures.

Continuing Legal Tech Education: Lifelong learning in legal technology will be essential. Lawyers will pursue ongoing education to stay updated on the latest tools, trends, and ethical considerations in technology-driven legal practice.

These predictions demonstrate that artificial intelligence and technology will revolutionize legal practice and communication, offering new opportunities for efficiency, client service, and innovation. Lawyers who embrace these technologies and adapt their skills accordingly will thrive in this evolving legal landscape.

C. PREPARING THE NEXT Generation of Lawyers for the Challenges and Opportunities Ahead:

To equip the next generation of lawyers for the evolving legal landscape, it's crucial to provide them with the skills, knowledge, and mindset necessary to navigate both challenges and opportunities. Here are key considerations for preparing future lawyers:

Technology Proficiency: Law schools should integrate technology training into their curricula. Students should become proficient in legal research tools, AI-powered software, data analytics, and cybersecurity practices.

Ethical Tech Use: Teach aspiring lawyers about the ethical use of technology, including issues related to privacy, bias in algorithms, and maintaining client confidentiality in digital environments.

Legal Tech Education: Offer specialized courses and workshops on legal technology and innovation. These programs should cover emerging technologies and their applications in legal practice.

Interdisciplinary Education: Encourage interdisciplinary learning by collaborating with other departments, such as computer science, business, or environmental studies. This fosters a holistic understanding of complex legal issues.

Embrace Online Learning: Incorporate online and blended learning models to prepare students for remote work and virtual court proceedings, which may become standard in the future.

Client-Centric Training: Stress the importance of client-centered communication, focusing on active listening, empathy, and clear, accessible language. Training should prepare lawyers to provide exceptional client service.

Cultural Competency: Develop cultural competency programs that help lawyers understand the diverse backgrounds and perspectives of clients and colleagues. This enhances their ability to communicate effectively in a globalized world.

Legal Entrepreneurship: Foster an entrepreneurial mindset among law students, encouraging them to explore innovative legal solutions and consider alternative career paths beyond traditional law firms.

Embrace Sustainability: Integrate environmental and sustainability considerations into legal education. Future lawyers should understand the legal implications of climate change and sustainability practices.

Legal Ethics and Technology: Offer courses on the ethical use of technology in legal practice, addressing issues like client data protection, AI bias, and the responsible implementation of AI tools.

Soft Skills Development: Emphasize soft skills such as negotiation, conflict resolution, and emotional intelligence, which are essential for effective communication and client advocacy.

Mentorship Programs: Establish mentorship programs that connect law students with experienced practitioners. These relationships can provide valuable guidance on adapting to the changing legal landscape.

Clinical Programs: Expand clinical programs and internships that allow students to gain practical experience using cutting-edge legal technology and communication platforms.

Continuing Education: Encourage lifelong learning and participation in continuing legal education programs. Lawyers should stay updated on technological advancements and ethical considerations throughout their careers.

Diversity and Inclusion: Promote diversity and inclusion in legal education to ensure that the legal profession reflects the diverse communities it serves. Diverse perspectives enhance problem-solving and communication.

Global Legal Awareness: Educate students about international law and global legal issues, preparing them for cross-border legal work and global challenges.

Leadership and Advocacy: Encourage students to develop leadership skills and engage in advocacy for causes they are passionate about. These experiences can enhance their communication abilities and impact.

By preparing the next generation of lawyers with a strong foundation in technology, ethics, communication, and adaptability, legal education can empower them to embrace the opportunities and overcome the challenges presented by the evolving legal landscape. This will not only benefit the future lawyers themselves but also the clients and communities they serve.

IX. Practical Exercises and Tips

"Practical Exercises and Tips" refer to hands-on activities and actionable advice designed to help individuals develop specific skills, improve their knowledge, or achieve practical goals in various domains. These exercises and tips are typically aimed at enhancing proficiency, problem-solving abilities, and practical application of knowledge or techniques. They can be utilized in a wide range of contexts, including education, professional development, self-improvement, and skill-building. Here's a breakdown of these components:

Practical Exercises: These are structured activities or tasks that individuals engage in to gain practical experience and improve their skills. Practical exercises often involve real-world scenarios or simulations that allow participants to apply theoretical knowledge in a hands-on manner. They are designed to reinforce learning and build competence through practice.

Tips: Tips are concise, actionable pieces of advice or recommendations that provide guidance on how to perform tasks more effectively, efficiently, or skillfully. They are often based on best practices, expert insights, or proven strategies and are intended to help individuals achieve better results or overcome common challenges.

Practical exercises and tips are valuable tools for learning and development because they bridge the gap between theory and practice, helping individuals acquire and refine practical skills. Whether it's mastering a new language, improving public speaking abilities, honing technical expertise, or enhancing problem-solving skills, practical exercises and tips provide actionable steps for individuals to achieve their goals and succeed in their endeavors.

A. Voice Training Exercises for Lawyers:

Voice training is essential for lawyers as effective communication is at the core of their profession. Lawyers must convey authority, clarity, and professionalism through their voices, whether in the courtroom, during negotiations, or in client meetings. Here are some voice training exercises tailored for lawyers:

Breath Control and Diaphragmatic Breathing:

Exercise: Practice deep breathing exercises to strengthen your diaphragm. Inhale deeply through your nose, allowing your abdomen to expand, and exhale slowly through your mouth. Repeat several times.

Tip: Diaphragmatic breathing provides better breath control, helping you project your voice with confidence and avoid vocal strain.

Pitch Control:

Exercise: Hum a comfortable note and gradually slide your pitch up and down, exploring your vocal range. Repeat this exercise, focusing on maintaining a steady pitch.

Tip: Developing pitch control allows you to vary your tone appropriately during communication to convey different emotions and emphasis.

Articulation and Diction:

Exercise: Pronounce tongue twisters or challenging phrases slowly and clearly. Example: "She sells seashells by the seashore."

Tip: Improved articulation and diction enhance your speech clarity, making it easier for others to understand your arguments.

Volume Control:

Exercise: Read a passage from a legal document or a book while gradually increasing and decreasing your volume. Practice speaking loudly and softly.

Tip: Volume control is crucial for addressing different courtroom sizes and maintaining audience engagement.

Tongue and Lip Exercises:

Exercise: Perform tongue twisters that involve precise tongue and lip movements, such as "red leather, yellow leather" or "unique New York."

Tip: These exercises help develop clear and precise pronunciation.

Voice Projection:

Exercise: Stand at one end of a room and practice speaking clearly to the farthest corner. Focus on projecting your voice without shouting.

Tip: Effective voice projection ensures that everyone in the room can hear you without straining.

Monotone Avoidance:

Exercise: Read a passage with varying emphasis on different words and phrases. Experiment with changing your pitch and tone to avoid a monotonous delivery.

Tip: Using intonation and emphasis makes your speech more engaging and persuasive.

Record and Review:

Exercise: Record your voice while practicing legal arguments or presentations. Listen to the recording and evaluate your clarity, tone, and articulation.

Tip: Self-assessment through recordings allows you to identify areas for improvement.

Warm-Up Exercises:

Exercise: Before important speaking engagements, perform vocal warm-up exercises like humming, lip trills, or tongue rolls to relax your vocal cords.

Tip: Warm-ups prevent voice strain and ensure your voice is ready for effective communication.

Public Speaking Practice:

Exercise: Practice delivering legal arguments or speeches in front of colleagues, mentors, or in a mock courtroom setting. Seek feedback for improvement.

Tip: Frequent public speaking practice builds confidence and hones your delivery skills.

Consistent practice of these voice training exercises can help lawyers enhance their vocal presence, improve communication skills, and become more effective advocates for their clients in various legal contexts.

B. Tips for Effective Communication in Legal Settings:

Effective communication is fundamental for lawyers in legal settings, whether in courtrooms, client meetings, negotiations, or written documents. Here are some essential tips to enhance communication in the legal profession:

Clarity and Precision:

Express legal concepts and arguments clearly and concisely, avoiding jargon and legalese whenever possible.

Define terms or concepts that may be unfamiliar to clients or the court.

Active Listening:

Pay close attention to clients, witnesses, and opposing counsel to fully understand their perspectives.

Ask clarifying questions to ensure comprehension and demonstrate your engagement.

Empathy and Rapport:

Build rapport with clients by showing empathy and understanding their concerns, emotions, and objectives.

Maintain professionalism and respect, even in contentious situations.

Preparation:

Thoroughly prepare for all legal proceedings, including researching case law, understanding statutes, and anticipating opposing arguments.

Familiarity with the facts and law will boost your confidence and credibility.

Structured Arguments:

Organize your arguments logically, using clear headings and subheadings in written documents.

In oral arguments, follow a structured outline to ensure a coherent and persuasive presentation.

Visual Aids:

Use visual aids like charts, graphs, and exhibits to clarify complex information during presentations or trials.

Ensure that visuals are well-prepared and add value to your communication.

Timing and Pacing:

Manage your speaking pace, allowing time for listeners to absorb information.

Avoid speaking too quickly or too slowly, which can hinder comprehension.

Body Language:

Maintain confident and professional body language, including eye contact, posture, and gestures.

Body language should align with your message and convey credibility.

Respect for Courtroom Etiquette:

Follow courtroom etiquette, including standing when addressing the judge, addressing opposing counsel respectfully, and adhering to dress codes.

Show deference to the court's rules and procedures.

Use of Technology:

Utilize technology effectively, such as PowerPoint presentations, video conferencing, and electronic document management systems.

Ensure that all technology functions smoothly and is compatible with the legal setting.

Document Clarity:

Draft legal documents with clarity and precision, using plain language where appropriate.

Use headings, bullet points, and formatting to make complex documents more reader-friendly.

Transparency:

Be transparent with clients about legal costs, potential outcomes, and the progress of their cases.

Manage client expectations by providing realistic assessments.

Adaptability:

Adapt your communication style to suit your audience, whether it's a judge, client, jury, or opposing counsel.

Tailor your approach based on the context and individuals involved.

Confidence and Poise:

Project confidence in your communication, but avoid arrogance.

Maintain composure, even when facing challenging situations or opposing arguments.

Continual Improvement:

Seek feedback from mentors, colleagues, or clients to continually refine your communication skills.

Attend communication workshops or courses to enhance your abilities.

Legal Ethics:

Uphold ethical standards in all communication, ensuring attorney-client privilege and confidentiality.

Avoid any conduct that may compromise your professional integrity.

Effective communication is not only a skill but also a critical tool for achieving positive legal outcomes and serving the best interests of clients. Lawyers who master these communication tips are better equipped to advocate persuasively, build strong client relationships, and navigate the complexities of the legal profession.

C. RESOURCES AND TOOLS for Continued Improvement in Legal Communication:

Continual improvement in legal communication is essential for lawyers to excel in their profession. Here are various resources and tools that can aid in ongoing development:

Professional Organizations:

Join legal associations like the American Bar Association (ABA) or your country's equivalent. These organizations often offer resources, publications, and training opportunities related to legal communication.

Legal Communication Workshops:

Attend workshops and seminars focused on legal communication, presentation skills, and effective advocacy. These are often offered by legal education providers or professional development organizations.

Public Speaking Courses:

Enroll in public speaking courses or workshops to enhance your oral communication skills, including voice modulation, pacing, and presence.

Legal Writing Guides:

Consult authoritative legal writing guides such as "The Bluebook" (for legal citation) and "The Elements of Style" by Strunk and White (for general writing principles).

Legal Technology Tools:

Familiarize yourself with legal technology tools that can improve communication, such as legal research platforms (e.g., Westlaw, LexisNexis), document management software, and AI-powered writing assistants.

Online Courses:

Explore online courses and certifications on platforms like Coursera, edX, and LinkedIn Learning that offer legal communication and writing courses.

Legal Communication Books:

Read books on legal communication, such as "Point Made: How to Write Like the Nation's Top Advocates" by Ross Guberman or "Win Your Case: How to Present, Persuade, and Prevail" by Gerry Spence.

Mentorship Programs:

Seek out mentorship opportunities within your law firm or through legal associations. Experienced mentors can provide valuable guidance on communication skills.

Feedback and Evaluation:

Solicit feedback from colleagues, supervisors, or mentors after presentations, trials, or written submissions. Constructive feedback is essential for improvement.

Continuing Legal Education (CLE):

Attend CLE programs that focus on legal communication, oral advocacy, and persuasive writing. Many bar associations offer CLE opportunities.

Professional Coaches:

Consider working with a professional communication coach who specializes in helping lawyers improve their communication skills, both written and verbal.

Podcasts and Webinars:

Listen to legal podcasts and attend webinars that discuss effective legal communication techniques, strategies, and case studies.

Bar Journals and Publications:

Stay informed by reading bar association journals, legal publications, and articles on legal communication trends and best practices.

Legal Writing Software:

Utilize legal writing software tools that provide style and grammar suggestions, such as ProWritingAid or Grammarly's Legal Writing Assistant.

Networking and Peer Support:

Connect with fellow lawyers through networking events, legal conferences, or online forums to share insights, experiences, and tips for improving communication.

Courtroom Observation:

Observe experienced lawyers in action by attending court sessions. Witnessing effective courtroom communication can provide valuable lessons.

Case Study Analysis:

Analyze notable legal cases and their communication strategies, including how arguments were presented and how written documents were structured.

Online Legal Communities:

Participate in online legal communities, such as LinkedIn legal groups or legal-focused subreddits, to engage in discussions on communication-related topics.

Voice Training Apps:

Use voice training apps that offer exercises and tips for improving vocal clarity, projection, and tone.

Legal Writing Clinics:

If available, participate in legal writing clinics offered by law schools or legal organizations. These provide opportunities for practical guidance on improving writing skills.

Remember that improvement in legal communication is an ongoing process. Combining these resources and tools with consistent practice and self-assessment can lead to significant enhancements in your ability to communicate effectively as a lawyer.

Conclusion

In conclusion, the power of effective communication lies at the heart of a lawyer's success in the legal profession. From the courtroom to client consultations, negotiations, and written submissions, the lawyer's voice is a potent tool for advocating, persuading, and achieving justice.

This book, "Lawyer in the Black Coat: The Power of Voice," delves into the profound influence of a lawyer's voice in the legal world. It uncovers the intricacies of the legal profession, highlighting the lawyer's role as a communicator and advocate. From mastering the art of oratory to harnessing the power of persuasion, lawyers are equipped with the skills to navigate the complex legal landscape.

The historical significance of the black coat symbolizes the lawyer's commitment to justice and the responsibilities that come with it. This book explores the symbolism of the black coat and its enduring relevance in the legal world.

Throughout its chapters, this book provides definitions, explanations, and insights into various aspects of legal communication, from the art of oratory and the psychology of persuasion to the challenges lawyers face and the evolving landscape of legal advocacy.

It offers practical exercises and tips for lawyers to enhance their communication skills and provides a wealth of resources and tools for continued improvement. Preparing the next generation of lawyers for the challenges and opportunities ahead is a central theme, emphasizing the importance of lifelong learning and adaptability.

As the legal profession evolves, lawyers must embrace technology, adapt to changing communication platforms, and uphold the highest ethical standards. The future of legal advocacy is dynamic, driven by artificial intelligence, globalized legal services, and the need for effective communication in diverse contexts.

In a world where communication is power, lawyers in their black coats are entrusted with the power of voice to advocate for justice, champion their clients' causes, and uphold the rule of law. Through continuous learning, self-improvement, and a commitment to ethical advocacy, lawyers can harness this power to create a more just and equitable society.

A. THE ENDURING IMPORTANCE of a Lawyer's Voice in an Ever-Changing World:

In a world marked by constant change and evolution, the importance of a lawyer's voice remains steadfast and enduring. Here are some key reasons why a lawyer's voice continues to be crucial in our ever-changing society:

Advocacy for Justice: Lawyers are the champions of justice, and their voices serve as a powerful tool to advocate for the rights and interests of their clients. In an ever-changing world, where new legal challenges constantly emerge, lawyers play a pivotal role in upholding the rule of law and ensuring that justice is served.

Effective Communication: Effective communication is a timeless skill that lawyers must possess. Whether it's presenting arguments in court, negotiating settlements, or advising clients, the ability to articulate ideas clearly and persuasively remains indispensable, regardless of technological advancements.

Adapting to Technological Changes: While technology has transformed the legal profession, lawyers are still responsible for interpreting and applying the law. Their voices guide clients through the complexities of legal tech, helping them understand the implications of automation, AI, and other innovations.

Ethical Advocacy: In a world where ethical considerations are increasingly vital, lawyers are entrusted with upholding ethical standards in their practice. Their voices speak for ethical conduct, ensuring that the legal profession maintains its integrity and accountability.

Navigating Globalization: As the world becomes more interconnected, lawyers must navigate international laws and cross-border legal issues. Their voices serve as a bridge between different legal systems and cultures, facilitating global cooperation and understanding.

Diverse Perspectives: Lawyers bring diverse perspectives to legal issues, ensuring that the law evolves to meet the needs of an ever-changing society. Their voices contribute to the development of laws that are relevant, fair, and just.

Access to Justice: In a world where disparities in access to justice persist, lawyers play a critical role in advocating for equal rights and opportunities. Their voices can be a powerful force for addressing systemic inequalities and ensuring that justice is accessible to all.

Public Policy and Legislation: Lawyers are often involved in shaping public policy and legislation. Their voices influence the creation of laws that address contemporary challenges, from environmental issues to technology regulation.

Human Rights and Social Justice: Lawyers are at the forefront of defending human rights and promoting social justice. Their voices are instrumental in fighting against discrimination, advocating for marginalized communities, and ensuring that fundamental rights are protected.

Education and Mentorship: Lawyers continue to educate and mentor the next generation of legal professionals. Their voices pass on the knowledge, values, and skills necessary to navigate the ever-changing legal landscape.

In conclusion, a lawyer's voice is an enduring and essential force in the legal profession and society at large. It serves as a beacon of justice, a source of ethical guidance, and a catalyst for positive change in an ever-evolving world. As long as there is a need for fairness, accountability, and the protection of rights, the lawyer's voice will remain a cornerstone of our legal system and a driving force for progress.

Also by Swatantra Bahadur

Breaking Barriers: LGBTQ Rights and Social Justice
Blossom with confidence
"Depression: A Roller Coaster Ride"
Finding Your Voice
Rahul Gandhi: The Untold Story
100 Aspects on Nature
Love By An Introvert
Man Of Golden India "Narendra Modi"
India " Unity lies in Diversity"
Indian's Heritage of Kashi "Varanasi"
"The Power of Voice: Lawyer in a Black Coat,"